BRANCH LINES
AROUND
DENBIGH

Vic Mitchell and Keith Smith

MP Middleton Press

Front cover: Ruthin was photographed in August 1959, as the locomotive passes the signal box and runs round its train. (Colour-Rail.com)

Back cover upper: Scenic joys were numerous in the area, as seen at Bodfari on 30th September 1961, while the locomotive blows off, waiting for the photographer. (A.M.Davies)

Back cover lower: It is November 1961 at Denbigh and we can enjoy the array of ageing semaphore signals alongside the recent signal box of modern styling. (A.M.Davies)

ACKNOWLEDGEMENTS

We are very grateful for the assistance received from many of those mentioned in the credits also to B.Bennett, A.R.Carder, G.Croughton, S.C.Jenkins, S.G.Jones, J.P.McCrickard, N.Langridge, B.Lewis, Mr D. and Dr S.Salter, S.Vincent and in particular, our always supportive wives, Barbara Mitchell and Janet Smith.

Published October 2012

ISBN 978 1 908174 32 1

© Middleton Press, 2012

Design Deborah Esher

Published by
     Middleton Press
     Easebourne Lane
     Midhurst
     West Sussex
     GU29 9AZ
Tel: 01730 813169
Fax: 01730 812601
Email: info@middletonpress.co.uk
www.middletonpress.co.uk

Printed in the United Kingdom by Henry Ling Limited, at the Dorset Press, Dorchester, DT1 1HD

CONTENTS

INDEX

I.   Railway Clearing House map 1947.

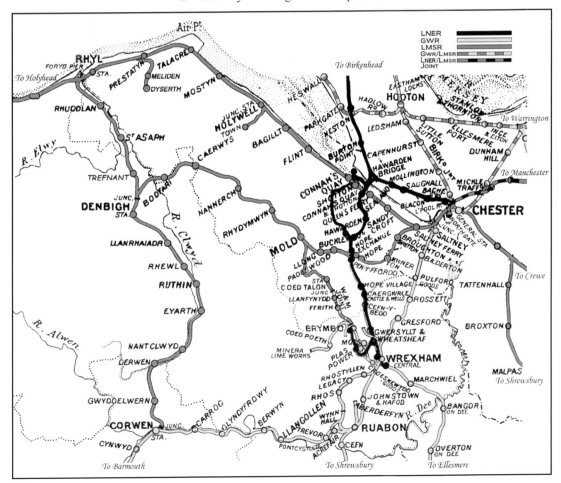

GEOGRAPHICAL SETTING

The coming of the railway to the Mold area caused the local coalfield to develop and also an oil industry, as the oil was distilled from cannel coal. The latter diminished in the 1870s, due to imported oil; the former declined in the 1930s, mainly due to competition from larger coalfields.

II. The 1946 edition at 4 miles to 1inch shows Saltney Ferry station below the word CHESTER right. Rhyl is top left and Corwen lower left, while Brymbo is three miles northwest of Wrexham. The boundary of England and Wales is shown with plus signs and dots.

Roughly parallel to the north-south coal measures is an outcrop of millstone grit and close to this is a band of limestone of great commercial value, particularly to the iron and steel industries. Parallel to this is the lofty outcrop of the Clwydian Range, which is composed of a different type of limestone. There was also nearby a three-mile wide band of small lead and zinc deposits.

The Clwyd Valley is the main feature west of this. The Afon Clwyd rises north of Corwen and flows into Liverpool Bay, west of Rhyl. The railway was close to it, except for the southern four miles or so. At Corwen is the east flowing River Dee, which turns north to pass through Chester. The watershed is near Nannerch.

The lines were built in Flintshire and Denbighshire, apart from five miles in Merionethshire, near Corwen, and ½ mile north of Kinnerton. Thus they were almost entirely in Wales, but that short length was in Cheshire. Ruthin was the county town of Denbighshire, while Mold served Flintshire.

The maps are to the scale of 25ins to 1 mile, with north at the top unless otherwise indicated. Furthermore as Welsh spelling and hyphenation has varied over the years we have generally used the form of the period.

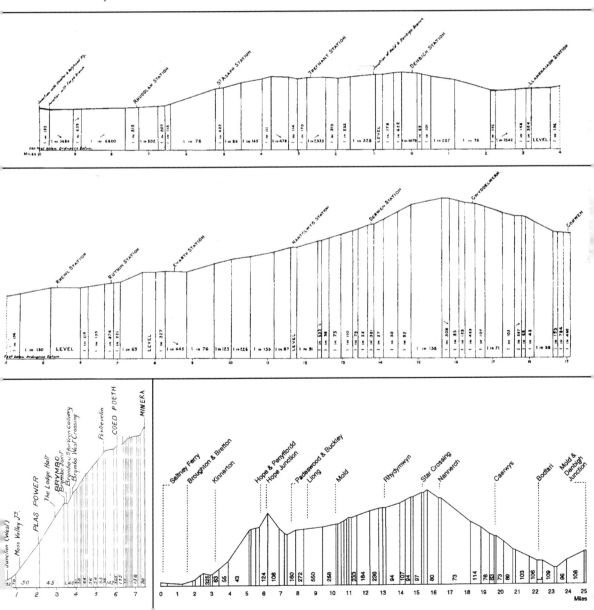

HISTORICAL BACKGROUND

The Chester & Holyhead Railway opened along the north coast of Wales in 1848 and an Act of 9th July 1847 allowed the Mold Railway to build a branch from it to Mold. It was taken over by the C&HR in 1848 and opened on 14th August 1849.

The next branch was from Rhyl to Denbigh, this being completed by the Vale of Clwyd Railway on 5th October 1858. Its Act was dated 23rd June 1856.

The Mold & Denbigh Junction Railway joined those two towns on 6th September 1869. The line south to Ruthin was authorised on 23rd July 1860 and was opened by the Denbigh, Ruthin & Corwen Railway on 1st March 1862. It was extended to Corwen on 6th October 1864. Here it met the 1865 route from Llangollen, which went on to Llandrillo in 1866. These two lines became part of the Great Western Railway in 1896. The London & North Western Railway controlled the VoCR from 1867 and the DR&CR from 1879. It worked the lines north of Corwen from their opening.

The LNWR absorbed the C&HR in 1859 and it became part of the London Midland & Scottish Railway in 1923, as did the M&DJR. The Wrexham, Mold & Connah's Quay Railway made a junction with the C&HR's Mold branch in 1866, near Hope. The WM&CQR became part of the Great Central Railway in 1905 and the London & North Eastern Railway in 1923.

Upon nationalisation in 1948, the LNER lines became part of the Eastern Region of British Railways, while the LMSR ones went into the London Midland Region and the Great Western Railway formed the Western Region. The area covered by this album was moved to the latter in 1963.

Closures to regular passenger services were as follows: Corwen to Denbigh 2nd February 1953, Rhyl to Denbigh 19th September 1955 and Saltney Ferry to Denbigh 30th April 1962. The Rhyl to Corwen section was used for Summer tourist trains until the Autumn of 1961. Freight withdrawals are given for each station in the captions, but the route west from Saltney Ferry remained open to Hope Junction until 2nd February 1970. Chemicals continued to be taken to the Synthite Works, west of Mold, until 15th March 1983.

Brymbo Branch

The C&HR opened the Ffrith branch for coal traffic from Padeswood on 14th September 1849; it was extended south to Brymbo on 27th January 1872 by the LNWR, although the southern three of the four miles were a joint venture with the GWR. The former built a mineral line between Mold and Coed Talon in 1869-70, it lasting until 1963. The line from Brymbo to Wrexham was opened by the Wrexham & Minera Railway for freight on 27th January 1872 and became a joint operation (LNWR and GWR). This section had a passenger service from 24th May 1882, while Mold to Coed Talon had a service from 1st August 1892 and the route north of Brymbo had one from 2nd May 1898. The former closed on 1st January 1931 and the latter on 27th March 1950.

March 1850

MOLD BRANCH.—Chester and Holyhead.

Down.	1 & 2 gov.	1 & 2 class.	1 2 3 class.	Up.	1 & 2 gov.	1 & 2 class.	1 2 3 class.
	morn	aft	aft		morn	aft	aft
Chester d.	10 45	3 0	5 30	Mold..dep.	9 40	12 30	4 0
Broughton..	10 56	3 11	5 41	Llong	9 45	12 35	4 5
Hope	11 14	3 29	5 59	Hope	9 54	12 44	4 14
Llong	11 19	3 34	6 4	Broughton..	10 9	12 59	4 29
Mold..arr.	11 25	3 40	6 10	Chester ar	10 20	1 10	4 40

ON SUNDAYS—From Chester at 9 40 a.m., 4 40 p.m.
From Mold at 8½ a.m., 3 20 p.m.
Fares—Chester to Mold, 1st cl. 2s. 6d.; 2nd, 1s. 9d.; 3rd, 1s. 6d.; gov., 1s. 1d.

June 1869

Crewe, Chester, Bangor, Carnarvon,

All 1 & 2 g]   MOLD BRANCH.—Chester and Holyhead—London and North Western.

Fares.	Down.	Week Days.			Sndys	Up.	Week Days.			Sndys

PASSENGER SERVICES

There were three weekday trains between Chester and Mold by March 1850, six months after the opening. Sunday trains were rare and so the tables below show weekday frequencies only. However, one or two trains ran on Sundays between Chester and Mold around 1880. Those running on less than four days per week are not shown.

	From Rhyl	Mold route	From Corwen
1865	5	5	4
1880	6	6	5
1910	10	11	5
1935	12	13	6
1952	10	10	6
1955	5	9	-
1961	-	9	-

Brymbo Branch

A service of three weekday trains ran between Mold and Coed Talon from 1893. It was extended to Brymbo in 1898. By 1929, there were four trips, but by 1949 it was down to two, Mondays to Fridays only. Again, no Sunday trains were found.

CHESTER, MOLD, DENBIGH, RUTHIN, CORWEN, and RHYL.—London and North Western.

April 1880

MOLD and BRYMBO (One class only).—L. M. & S. and G. W.

E Except Saturdays.   S Saturdays only.

July 1929

January 1935

RHYL, ST. ASAPH, and DENBIGH

1. From Rhyl

RHYL

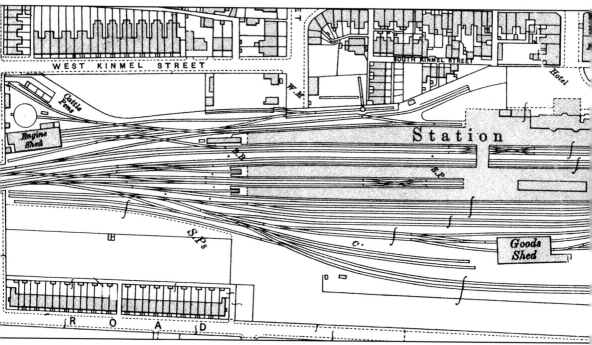

III.   The 1912 edition is at 20ins to 1 mile and it features the two bay platforms used by Vale of Clwyd trains to Denbigh and Corwen. The 50ft turntable (top left) was replaced by a 60ft one in 1938.

1.   This is a view west from Vale Road from about 1920 and it includes the main buildings on the right and a glazed weather screen near the coaches. Passengers had full protection from the weather on the footbridge after the rebuilding of the station in the late 1870s. (Stations UK)

2.   The engine shed was photographed on 14th September 1952, when its code was 6K. In attendance are nos 40580, 42663 and 41120; there were 27 locomotives here in 1950. The shed closed on 11th February 1963, having been re-roofed in about 1938. (R.S.Carpenter)

3.   The north facade was photographed in the rain in the Summer of 1956, when the Bristol double-decker was new. The canopy was demolished later, along with the equally fine shelter beyond it. (V.R.Anderson)

4.   The exhaust from a class 40 departing west on 3rd August 1968 partially obscures the former Vale of Clwyd bay platforms and the goods yard. On the left is No. 2 Box which had 126 levers and was in use from 1900 until 26th March 1960. Listed Grade II, it was still standing in 2012, as was No. 1, which was still in use. (Bentley coll.)

Other views can be found in *Chester to Rhyl* and *Rhyl to Bangor*. The latter contains details of the branch to Foryd Harbour and the nearby Kinmel Camp Railway.

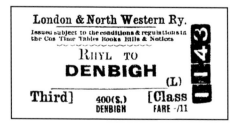

London & North Western Ry.

Issued subject to the conditions & regulations in the Cos Time Tables Books Bills & Notices

RHYL TO
DENBIGH (L)

Third]   [Class

400(S.)   FARE -/11
DENBIGH

0143

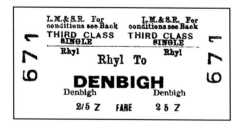

L.M.&S.R. For   L.M.&S.R. For
conditions see Back   conditions see Back

THIRD CLASS   **THIRD CLASS**
SINGLE   SINGLE

Rhyl   Rhyl

Rhyl To

DENBIGH
Denbigh   Denbigh

2/5 Z   FARE   2 5 Z

671   671

WEST OF RHYL

5.　　Rhyl is in the background as we look across the Afon Clwyd, the mouth of which is beyond the left border. Near this was Foryd Harbour, which was served by a siding until 1959. It ran behind the camera and passed under the four main lines, having diverged from the Vale of Clwyd route near the confluence of the two curved lines. The view is from the 56-lever signal box.
(Lens of Sutton coll.)

FORYD

6.　　The station was open until 20th April 1895, when it was replaced by one on the main line. However, this loop was retained to enable locomotives to run round Foryd Harbour freight trains. The junction is behind the camera. There was a 15-lever signal box until 1883 and a ground frame thereafter. The branch had a hand-worked level crossing over the A548, further north.
(Lens of Sutton coll.)

RHUDDLAN

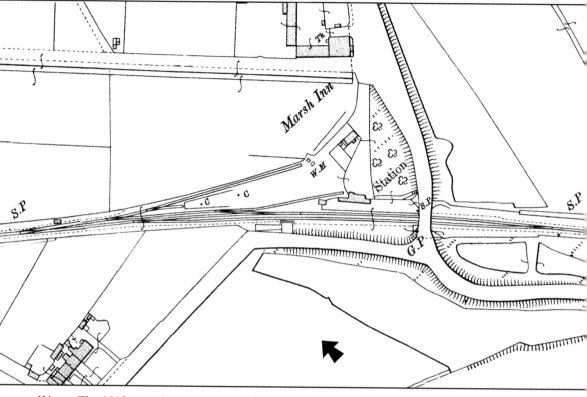

IV.   The 1913 map shows a road junction on the embankment, south of the bridge span. This had originally been on the site of the station. The population was 1333 in 1901, this rising to 2164 in 1961.

7.   A view towards Denbigh in about 1930 has the goods loop on the right. This remained in use until 2nd September 1956 and was controlled from an eight-lever ground frame on the platform. (C.Gilbert/R.S.Carpenter coll.)

8.　　　A photograph from July 1946 has three telephone wires giving the impression of scratches. The 4-4-0 is no. 646. which was classified 2P; plenty of boxes wait by the parcels shed. (Bentley coll.)

9.　　　A 1954 record from the bridge features imaginative garden borders and nameboard. A camping coach stands near the 5-ton crane; there had been four in 1948. The goods yard remained in use until 4th May 1964. (D.K.Jones coll.)

10.   A snap from a train on 27th August 1954 has the ground frame between the decency wall of the gents and the flower bed. The lantern would contain an oil lamp after dark and it would illuminate a rare display of the word STATION on a station. (R.M.Casserley)

September 1952

Table 101   RHYL, ST. ASAPH, and DENBIGH

Week Days only

Miles		a.m	a.m		a.m	a.m	a.m	a.m	p.m	p.m	p.m		p.m	p.m	p.m		p.m		p.m
					S	E	S												S
—	Rhyl ....dep	5 20	7 40	..	8 25	1050	11 5	1145	1 41	2 43	4 12	..	5 5	23	7 10	..	9 25	..	1030
3¾	Rhuddlan	5 28	7 47	..	8 32	11 0	1112	1152	1 48	2 50	4 19	..	5 12	5 30	7 17	..	9 32	..	1037
6	St. Asaph	5 35	7 53	..	8 38	11 6	1119	1159	1 56	2 58	4 25	..	5 19	5 37	7 23	..	9 38	..	1043
8¼	Trefnant	5 41	8 0	..	8 45	1113	1125	12 7	2 3	3 6	4 32	..	5 28	5 43	7 30	..	9 44	..	1050
11	Denbigh ....arr	5 49	8 8	..	8 54	1121	1133	1215	2 11	3 14	4 42	..	5 33	5 52	7 33	..	9 52	..	1056

Week Days only

Miles		a.m	a.m		a.m	a.m	a.m	p.m	p.m	p.m	p.m	p.m		p.m	p.m	p.m	p.m
							E	S	E	H				S	S	E	
—	Denbigh ....dep	5 53	7 5	..	9 5	1010	1030	1210	1213	1 42	1 42	2 58	3 32	..	4 50	5 50	5 55	..	7 50
2¾	Trefnant	6 5	7 12	..	9 12	1017	..	1217	1220	1 49	1 49	3 5	3 39	..	4 57	5 57	6 2	..	7 57
5	St. Asaph	6 11	7 18	..	9 18	1023	..	1223	1226	1 55	1 55	3 11	3 45	..	5 3	6 3	6 8	..	8 3
7¼	Rhuddlan	6 16	7 23	..	9 23	1028	..	1228	1231	2 0	2 0	3 16	3 50	..	5 8	6 8	6 13	..	8 8
11	Rhyl ....arr	6 23	7 30	..	9 30	1035	1058	1235	1244	2 7	2 10	3 23	3 57	..	5 15	6 15	6 20	..	8 15

S 3 minutes later on Saturdays.   **E** Except Saturdays.   **H** Saturdays only. Through Carriage from Mold dep. 12 55 p.m.

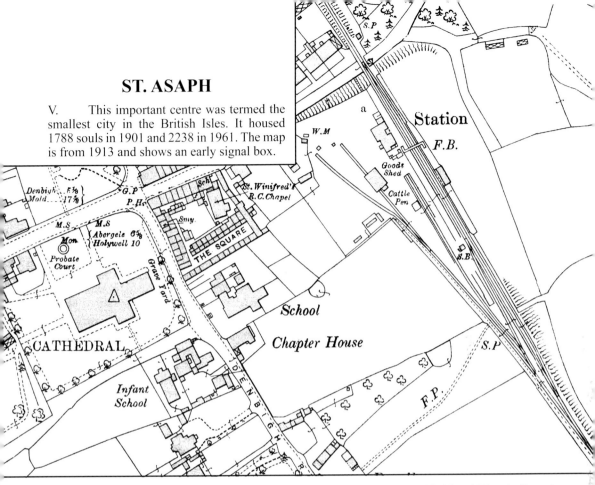

ST. ASAPH

V. This important centre was termed the smallest city in the British Isles. It housed 1788 souls in 1901 and 2238 in 1961. The map is from 1913 and shows an early signal box.

Denbigh... 5⅝
Mold... 17⅞

G.P.
P.H.
Sch.
St.Winifred's R.C.Chapel

Station
F.B.

W.M

Goods Shed

M.S
M.S
Abergele 6⅜
Holywell 10
Mon

Smy.

THE SQUARE

Cattle Pen

Probate Court

Grave Yard

S.B

CATHEDRAL

School

Chapter House

S.P

Infant School

D E N B I G H

F.P.

11. The platform and loop on the right of this northward view was added in 1877 and allowed passenger trains to pass. No. 42677 is on the bridge over Chester Street (A55 then), with the 12.10pm to Corwen on 11th April 1950. (R.S.Carpenter)

CROSS THE LINE BY THE BRIDGE

12.   Pleasing garden borders were pictured on 27th August 1954, along with threshing equipment at the end loading dock. North Wales Agricultural Equipment provided much traffic, as did the Vale of Clwyd Farmers Cooperative. A 15-lever frame was near the footbridge, its white levers being visible. (R.M.Casserley)

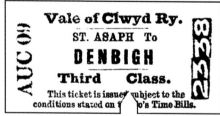

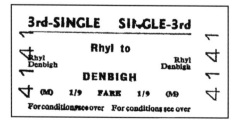

ST. ASAPH.

POPULATION, 2,063.

Telegraph station at Rhyl, 5¾ miles.

The city of St. Asaph is situated on a delightful eminence between the streams, near the confluence of the rivers Elwy and Clwyd. The principal attraction of this city is the *Cathedral*, which was first built of wood in 596, by St. Asaph, and rebuilt in 1770. The plan of the church is like most others cruciform, with a square embattled tower rising from the intersection of the nave and transepts. The visitor on entering the sacred edifice will be struck with the solemnity which pervades the building; the chastened light, entering from the richly painted windows, evidently copied from those of Tintern Abbey, throws a softened tint over the Gothic stalls and chequered pavement of the choir, which to the eye capable of appreciating the beauty of the scene is highly pleasing and interesting. It contains tombs of Bishops ap Owen in 1512, and Barrow, the uncle of the celebrated Boac Barrow. The most eminent prelates of this see were Parry, Morgan (who translated the Bible into Welsh), Tanner, Beveridge, and Horsley.

The *Episcopal Palace* is an ancient one, rebuilt by the late bishop. The neighbourhood of St. Asaph is studded with a variety of gentlemen's seats, among which are *Pengwern*, Lord Mostyn ; *Kinmel*, Lord Dinorben ; and *Bodelwyddan*, Sir J. Williams, Bart.

Extract from *Bradshaw's Guide* for 1866.
(Reprinted by Middleton Press 2011)

13. The loop was taken out of use on 2nd September 1956 and subsequently removed. Tourist trains continued for nine years after regular passenger services ceased and one example is seen on 6th June 1960 behind 2-6-4T no. 80091. (W.G.Rear/Bentley coll.)

14. This tour on 18th August 1960 is carrying the correct headboard "Cambrian Radio Cruise". It is on 4-6-0 no. 75054, a locomotive then based at Rhyl. A commentary on the passing scene was broadcast in each coach, a rare and popular treat. (W.G.Rear/Bentley coll.)

15.   Initially termed "Land Cruise", this train on 30th August 1961 has just one carriage board, but no headboard. Class 4MT 4-6-0 no. 75020 is on the bridge over the River Elwy, north of the station. The train varied over the years, but the route always included Barmouth and Bangor. (Bentley coll.)

16.   Running north on 30th August 1963 is ex-LMS 4-6-0 no. 44686, the 1877 platform being evident on the left. The goods yard was open until 4th May 1964. (Bentley coll.)

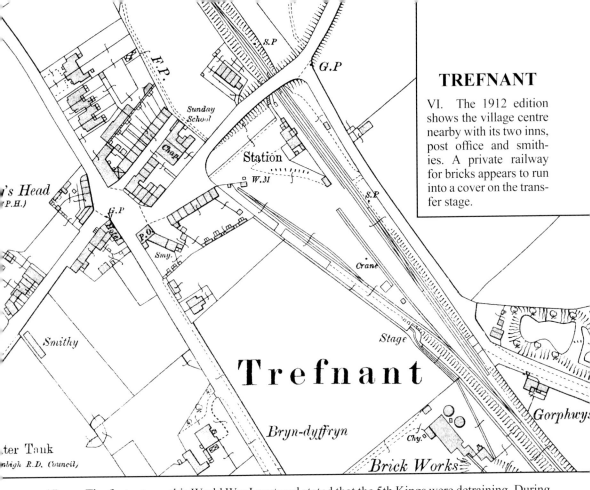

TREFNANT

VI. The 1912 edition shows the village centre nearby with its two inns, post office and smithies. A private railway for bricks appears to run into a cover on the transfer stage.

(map labels: F.P., S.P, G.P, Sunday School, Chap¹, Station, W.M, S.P, 's Head (P.H.), G.P, Hotel, P.O, Smy., Crane, Smithy, Stage, Trefnant, Bryn-dyffryn, Chy., Gorphwys, Brick Works, ter Tank, ...nbigh R.D. Council)

17.   The footnote on this World War I postcard stated that the 5th Kings were detraining. During World War II, the Royal Engineers laid three sidings south of the brickworks to serve an Army fuel depot and general storage site. The cattle dock was adjacent to the white shed to the left of the locomotive. (Lens of Sutton coll.)

18.   A classic postcard record includes the staff, plus a gloved man who appears to be a chauffeur. For many years, southbound trains stopped here for two minutes for ticket inspection. (P.Laming coll.)

19.   A 1955 panorama includes all the features which would eventually be demolished, including the bridge. A housing estate was built over the site. The rodding tunnel to the 11-lever signal frame is near the bridge. (D.K.Jones coll.)

20.   The jib of the 5-ton crane is visible in the goods yard, which was in use until 5th August 1967, later than the others further north. Beyond the goods shed is the chimney of the brickworks. (D.K.Jones coll.)

21.   The goods shed was still standing on 13th May 1965 as class 5 4-6-0 no. 45275 ran north. The loop had been taken out of use on 2nd September 1956. The two-storey building had formed the accommodation for the station master. (W.G.Rear/Bentley coll.)

SOUTH OF TREFNANT

22.   Chester trains ran on the left and our route is on the right in this September 1960 view south. This had been the site of Mold & Denbigh Junction until 28th April 1957, the single line from Rhyl joining double track from Mold. The 20-lever signal box closed and the two single lines were controlled from Denbigh thereafter. (W.G.Rear/Bentley coll.)

VII.   Published in 1962, this diagram includes many of the original names and shows some of the lines lifted by that time. (Railway Magazine)

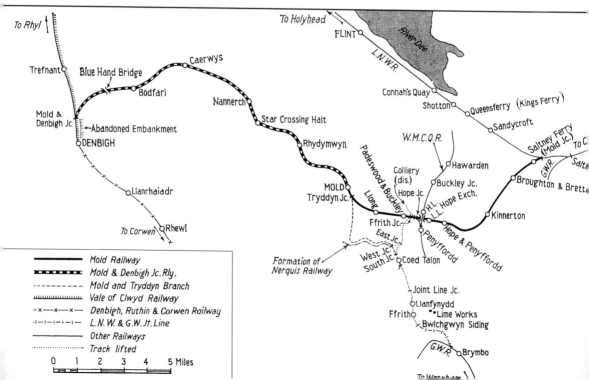

Legend:

───────	Mold Railway
▪▪▪▪▪▪▪▪	Mold & Denbigh Jc. Rly.
─ ─ ─ ─ ─	Mold and Tryddyn Branch
⊔⊔⊔⊔⊔	Vale of Clwyd Railway
─x─x─x─	Denbigh, Ruthin & Corwen Railway
─∙─∙─∙─	L.N.W. & G.W. Jt. Line
───────	Other Railways
············	Track lifted

0 1 2 3 4 5 Miles

2. From Saltney Ferry
SALTNEY FERRY

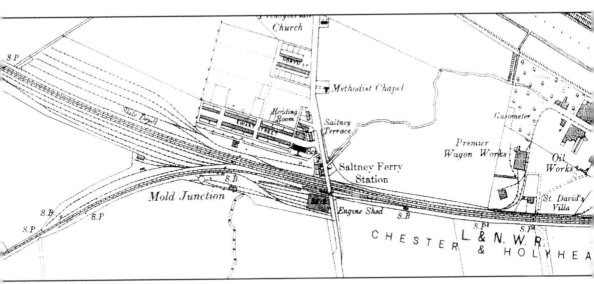

VIII.   The Chester to Holyhead main line of the LNWR is across this 1913 map, which is scaled at 6ins to 1 mile. The station opened over 40 years after the routes, on 1st January 1891 and quadrupling of the main line was completed in 1899. The houses were for railway staff and there were four signal boxes. The marshalling yard was in use from 1890 to 1979. There had been a south to west line to form a triangular junction for some years. This was a short single line connection between Mold Junction No. 3 box (on the Denbigh line) and Mold Junction Down Yard. However, it was not signalled for through running to/from the Holyhead main line, just shunting moves in and out of Mold Junction Yard. Hawarden Airfield was developed in that area during World War II.

23.   All three photographs are from about March 1962 and this view east shows that access to the island platform was direct from the road bridge, this having replaced a level crossing in 1874. The north wall of the engine shed is on the right. The code was 6B from 1935 until closure in April 1966. (Lens of Sutton coll.)

24.	We are on a train from Mold and are approaching the locomotive depot, which was completed in 1890. The 60ft turntable was beyond the right border and No. 2 Box is near the centre of the picture. (A.M.Davies)

Picture numbers 19 to 28 in our *Chester to Rhyl* album expand the coverage of this fascinating area.

25.	Moments later, we enter the platform and gain a glimpse of No.1 Box, which was in use from 1902 until 2005. It had a 60-lever frame until 1984 and a panel thereafter. Passenger traffic ceased here on 30th April 1963 and freight on 4th May 1964. (A.M.Davies)

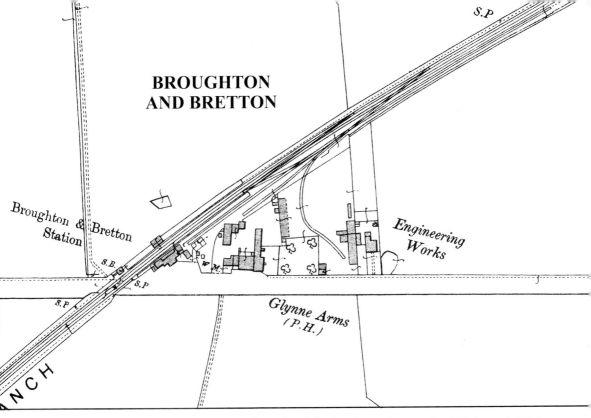

BROUGHTON AND BRETTON

IX.   The 1911 survey shows the small angle of the level crossing on the A55 (now A5104). There was a private siding for the Premier Artificial Stone Co. listed in 1938. The station was "Broughton Hall" in 1861-1908 and as above thereafter.

26.   A Chester to Denbigh train was recorded on 7th May 1959, while the main road to North Wales from Cheshire was closed. Passengers were served here from 14th August 1849 until 30th April 1962, although a service for workmen continued until 2nd September 1963. (H.F.Wheeller/R.S.Carpenter)

27.   Workers were destined to a massive airfield created north of the line in 1939, which was used for training and aircraft storage by the RAF and for aeroplane manufacture by Vickers Armstrong and later the de Havilland Aircraft Company. The latter continues. A private siding was provided and this 25-lever signal box served from 1939 to 2nd February 1970. (Stations UK)

28.   The station was well cared for during its use by Prime Minister Gladstone, who lived nearby. It is seen near to closure; goods traffic ceased on 4th May 1964. (Stations UK)

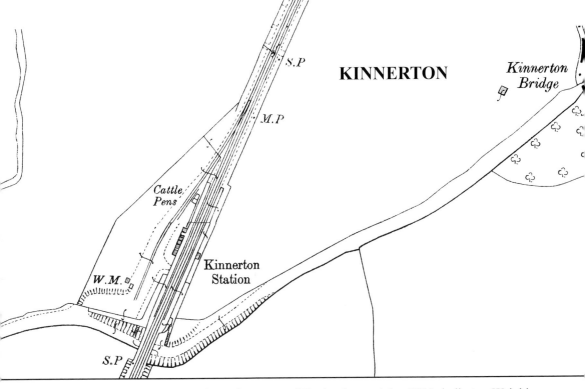

KINNERTON

S.P

M.P

Kinnerton Bridge

Cattle Pens

W.M.

Kinnerton Station

S.P

X.   The 1911 edition includes a fragment of England, top right. W.M. indicates Weighing Machine and steps are shown down into the cutting which took the road under the railway.

29.   LMS 4-4-0 no. 5361 is departing from the small station, which did not open until 2nd March 1891. It was provided with minimal facilities. (R.M.Casserley coll.)

30.　　Seen in March 1962 are the LNWR's factory-made buildings, now described as "flat-pack". The severe gradient meant that down trains could have a problem starting from here. (A.M.Davies)

31.　　It is April 1962 and nature is taking over, but soon all would be demolished. The goods yard could take 14 wagons and was closed on 5th December 1955. (D.K.Jones coll.)

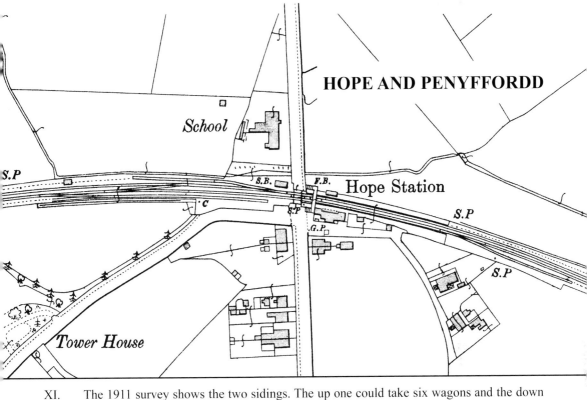

HOPE AND PENYFFORDD

School

S.P

S.B.   F.B.   Hope Station

C

S.P

G.P

S.P

S.P

Tower House

XI.   The 1911 survey shows the two sidings. The up one could take six wagons and the down one sixteen.

32.   It is August 1954 and the Hope gardens are in full bloom. The suffix had been added on 16th January 1912, the station being close to the centre of Penyffordd. (R.M.Casserley)

33.　　The signal box seen on 7th August 1957 had 15 levers and was in use from 12th March 1944 until 2nd February 1970. Its wheel worked the gates over the A550. The main building became a private house. (R.S.Carpenter)

34.　　Banking engines working from Mold Junction would be detached here, having climbed to over 300ft above sea level. The goods yard here closed on 5th September 1955; its crane was rated at one ton and is marked on the map with a C. (A.M.Davies)

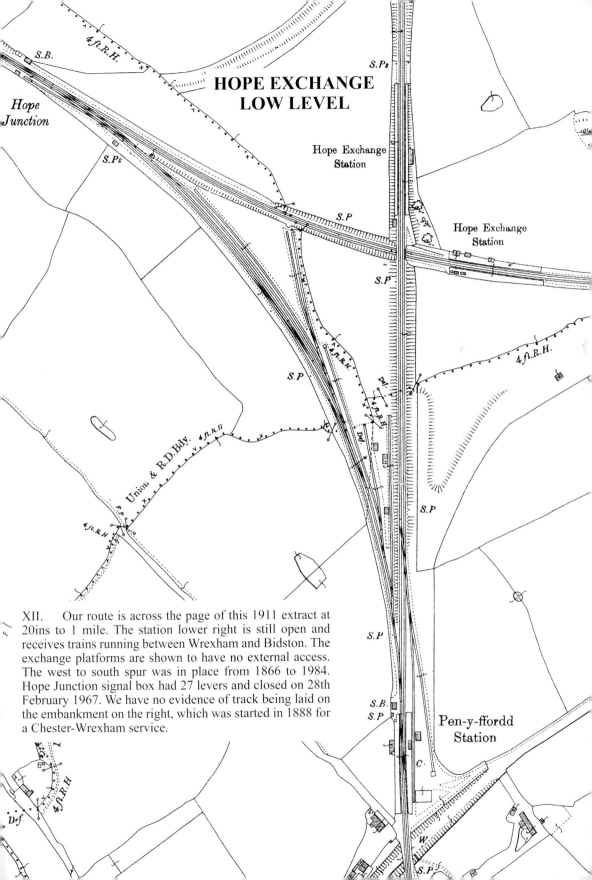

**HOPE EXCHANGE
LOW LEVEL**

*Hope
Junction*

S.B.

4 ft. R.H.

S.Ps

S.Ps

S.P

Hope Exchange
Station

S.Ps

Hope Exchange
Station

S.P

4 ft. R.H.

4 ft. R.H.

S.P

S.P

Def.

4 ft. R.H.

4 ft. R.H.

Def.

Union & R.D. Bdy.

4 ft. R.H.

F.Ps

4 ft. R.H.

S.P

XII.   Our route is across the page of this 1911 extract at
20ins to 1 mile. The station lower right is still open and
receives trains running between Wrexham and Bidston. The
exchange platforms are shown to have no external access.
The west to south spur was in place from 1866 to 1984.
Hope Junction signal box had 27 levers and closed on 28th
February 1967. We have no evidence of track being laid on
the embankment on the right, which was started in 1888 for
a Chester-Wrexham service.

S.P

S.B.
S.P

**Pen-y-ffordd
Station**

C.

4 ft. R.H.

W.

Def.

S.P.

35.   A westbound train from Chester in March 1962 is about to pass under the former LNER route. Two of the three huts on the down platform are visible; one had been a waiting room for ladies. A porter had been on duty here, mainly for parcel transfer. (A.M.Davies)

36.   A close up at about the same time shows a gate on the path to the platforms at High Level. The station was in use from 1868 until 1st September 1958 and the suffix was applied from 7th December 1953. There is no trace of it today. (Lens of Sutton coll.)

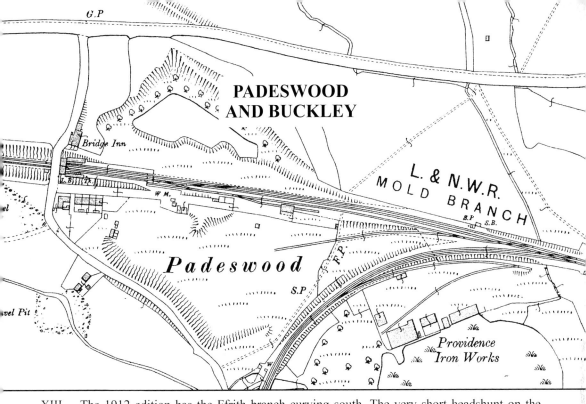

PADESWOOD
AND BUCKLEY

L. & N.W.R.
MOLD BRANCH

Padeswood

Providence
Iron Works

XIII.   The 1912 edition has the Ffrith branch curving south. The very short headshunt on the private siding was probably due to equine operation. The signal box was first known as Ffrith Junction and later as Padeswood Junction. The branch was in use from 14th September 1849 and was double track as far as Coppa Colliery. The route and box closed on 29th July 1934, following an accident that day. Derailed wagons damaged a bridge.

37.   A record from 1951 shows generous provision for gentlemen on both platforms and portable steps available for less agile passengers. The line climbs at 1 in 160 here. BUCKLEY was added to the name on 1st February 1894. (Stations UK)

38.   A photograph from 27th August 1954 reveals no passengers, but that the Bridge Inn is sinking into the marshland, shown on the map. The station closed before the line, on 6th January 1958 and was quickly demolished. The adjacent five staff dwellings survived and the goods yard was in use until 6th August 1956. (H.C.Casserley)

39.   No. 25168 is running near the site of the goods yard, which once had a shed with a siding through it. The tanks are bound for the Synthite Works near Mold on 18th September 1980. (T.Heavyside)

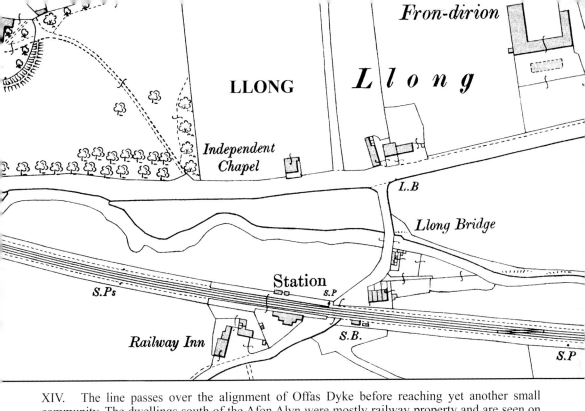

XIV.   The line passes over the alignment of Offas Dyke before reaching yet another small community. The dwellings south of the Afon Alyn were mostly railway property and are seen on the 1912 edition. There had been a private siding south of the signal box around 1900.

40.   This view is from a train bound for Chester on 27th August 1953. The frame replaced the 24-lever box shown on the map and was in use from the 1930s until 9th January 1966. (R.M.Casserley)

41.   The low platforms were the original ones and are seen in about 1959. As a wartime economy measure, the station was closed from 1st January 1917 until 5th May 1919. (Stations UK)

42.   A photograph from 18th September 1980 features no. 25168 with supplies for Synthite Sidings. The distant signal was fixed and acted as a caution sign. The four wooden gates had been replaced by two steel tubular ones, but they were still hand operated. The building was in residential use more than 30 years later. (T.Heavyside)

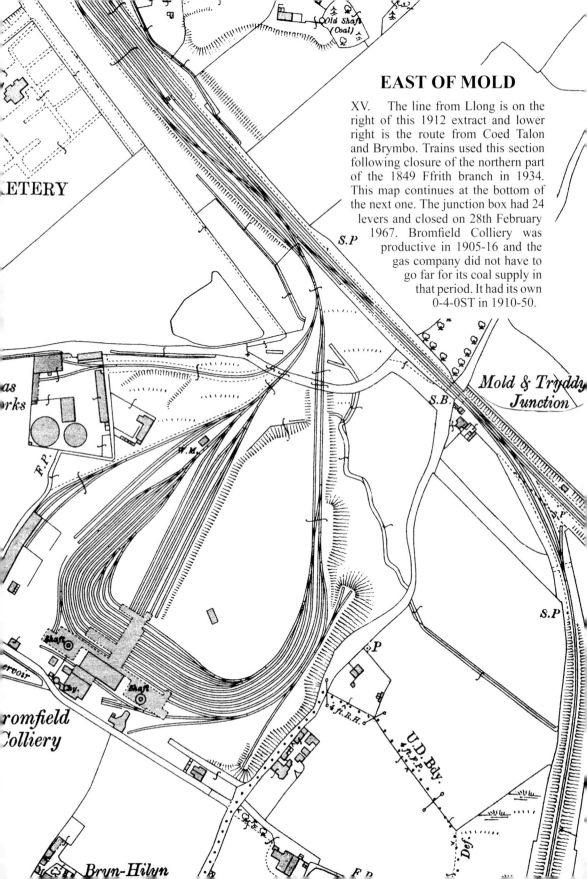

EAST OF MOLD

XV.   The line from Llong is on the right of this 1912 extract and lower right is the route from Coed Talon and Brymbo. Trains used this section following closure of the northern part of the 1849 Ffrith branch in 1934. This map continues at the bottom of the next one. The junction box had 24 levers and closed on 28th February 1967. Bromfield Colliery was productive in 1905-16 and the gas company did not have to go far for its coal supply in that period. It had its own 0-4-0ST in 1910-50.

ETERY

Old Shaft (Coal)

S.P

as rks

F.P.

W.M.

Mold & Tryddy Junction

S.B.

romfield Colliery

S.P

S.P

P

4 ft R.H.

U.D.Bdy.

4 ft F.P.

ervoir

Shaft

Sy.

Shaft

Def.

F.P.

Bryn-Hilyn

F.B.

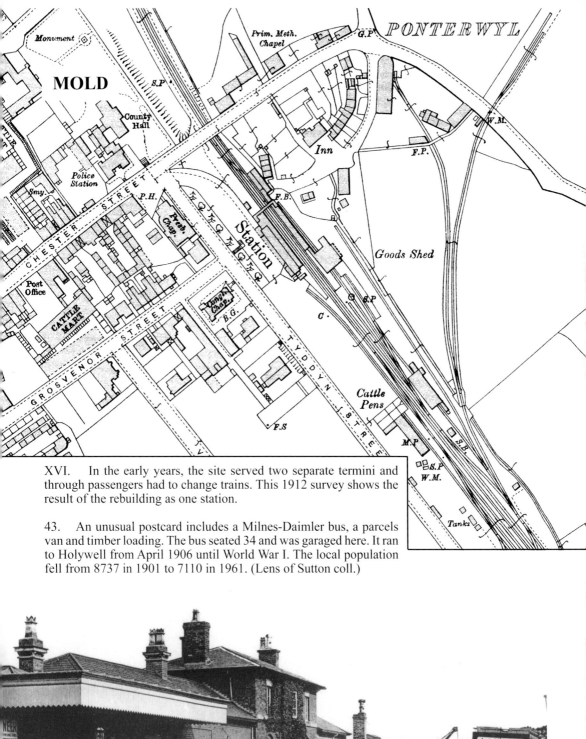

XVI.   In the early years, the site served two separate termini and through passengers had to change trains. This 1912 survey shows the result of the rebuilding as one station.

43.   An unusual postcard includes a Milnes-Daimler bus, a parcels van and timber loading. The bus seated 34 and was garaged here. It ran to Holywell from April 1906 until World War I. The local population fell from 8737 in 1901 to 7110 in 1961. (Lens of Sutton coll.)

44. Bidirectional running was possible, as seen on 2nd October 1955 as 2-6-4T no. 42461 waits with an RCTS railtour. It ran from Chester General via Dyserth, Rhyl, Corwen, Coed Talon, Hope Exchange, Wrexham Exchange and Shotton High Level to Chester Northgate.
(Lens of Sutton coll.)

45. No. 44595 has arrived from Coed Talon on 15th July 1963 and we have the opportunity to examine the architectural details, notably the great lengths of the canopies. Being the county town, it seems that a covered footbridge was deemed appropriate. The station site was cleared in 1988 to make way for a Tesco store. (R.M.Casserley)

46.   Beyond the goods shed on the left, part of the engine shed can be seen. This closed in 1890, when Mold Junction depot opened near Saltney Ferry. The shed was subsequently used as a grain warehouse. No. 25168 is on its way to the Synthite Sidings on 18th September 1980. The 35-lever flat roofed signal box had been beyond the sheds and closed on 28th February 1967. The goods traffic here ceased on 3rd April 1972. (T.Heavyside)

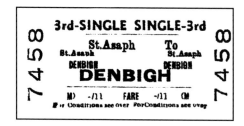

3rd-SINGLE SINGLE-3rd
7458   St.Asaph   7458
St.Asaph   To   St.Asaph
DENBIGH   DENBIGH
DENBIGH
M) -/11   FARE   -/11 CM
F·· Conditions see over For Conditions see over

D. R. & C. R.
RUTHIN   To
TREVOR
vi · Corwen &G. W. Ry.
Second   Class
This ticket is issued subject to the
conditions stated on the Co's time bills

→ 47. No. 25168 is returning from the Synthite Works on the same day and is approaching the first of two main road bridges over the line. It is a minor road in the background. (T.Heavyside)

48.   Less than a mile from Mold station was this box, which lasted until 8th August 1966. It is seen in September 1961. The works had been started in 1874 and it lasted until 1939. The site was used by the Ministry of Supply for storage until 1946. (W.G.Rear/ Bentleycoll.)

49.   Chemical production by Synthite Ltd began here in 1950 and initially it had a Barclay 0-4-0ST, with diesels following. Formaldehyde was the main output. Seen on 16th April 1965, this Simplex diesel was originally owned by the Lancashire & Yorkshire Railway, having been built in 1920. (A.Neale)

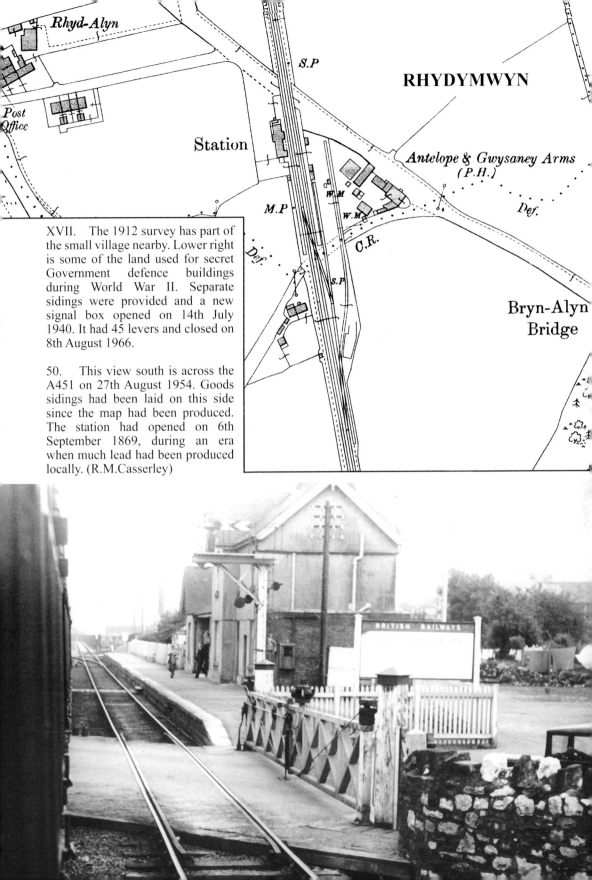

Rhyd-Alyn

Post Office

Station

S.P

RHYDYMWYN

Antelope & Gwysaney Arms
(P.H.)

M.P

W.M

W.M

Def.

C.R.

S.P

Def.

Bryn-Alyn Bridge

XVII.   The 1912 survey has part of the small village nearby. Lower right is some of the land used for secret Government defence buildings during World War II. Separate sidings were provided and a new signal box opened on 14th July 1940. It had 45 levers and closed on 8th August 1966.

50.   This view south is across the A451 on 27th August 1954. Goods sidings had been laid on this side since the map had been produced. The station had opened on 6th September 1869, during an era when much lead had been produced locally. (R.M.Casserley)

BRITISH RAILWAYS

51.   The vista from the other side of the train was recorded moments later. The wagon with spaced boards was for the conveyance of coke, a lightweight fuel. The goods yard closed on 4th May 1964; it had a 5-ton crane in its later years. (H.C.Casserley)

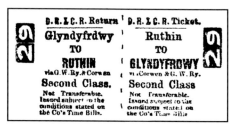

52.   The 4.15pm Denbigh to Mold train was hauled by BR 2-6-4T no. 80050 on 15th August 1957, while the staff crossing gleamed in the rain. The paraffin lamps were close to the ground, owing to their poor light output. (R.S.Carpenter)

53.   The down track was lifted from here northwards, after its closure on 12th May 1962. The photograph is from about 1965. The building was adapted as a house after traffic ceased. (D.K.Jones coll.)

WEST OF RHYDYMWYN

54.   After passing Dolfechlas Crossing Box (22-levers), trains descended to Hendre Sidings Box (20 levers), which is seen on 28th August 1961. Both closed on 12th May 1962. The leading coach is on a bridge over the River Wheeler, its valley being very narrow here. There were sidings on the route for Olwyn Goch lead mine, Ruby Brick & Lime Works and Hendre Quarry for limestone. (W.G.Rear/Bentley coll.)

STAR CROSSING

55.   The stop was near a rural crossroads and close to the summit of the route. It had the suffix HALT from its opening on 2nd November 1914 until 1929. It was closed in 1917-1919. The guard gives the right away on 28th August 1961, from an up train. "Star" was the name of a a nearby inn. (W.G.Rear/Bentley coll.)

56.   The building was home to the station master and contained a booking office. The down side lamp is seen in about 1962. The house was not demolished. Cilcain was the nearest village and it was 1½ miles to the south. (D.K.Jones coll.)

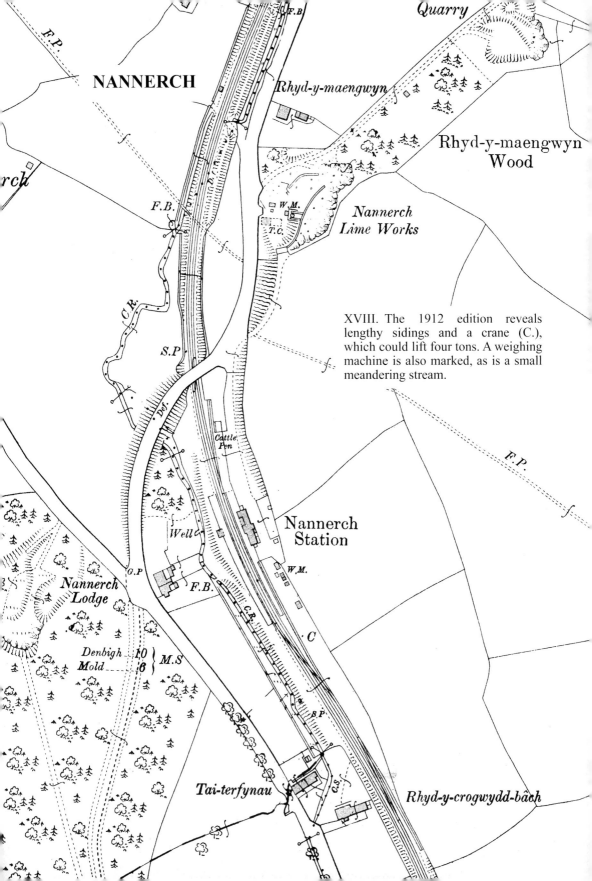

NANNERCH

Quarry

Rhyd-y-maengwyn

Rhyd-y-maengwyn
Wood

F.P.

F.B.

rch

W.M.

T.C.

*Nannerch
Lime Works*

F.B.

C.B.

S.P.

XVIII. The 1912 edition reveals
lengthy sidings and a crane (C.),
which could lift four tons. A weighing
machine is also marked, as is a small
meandering stream.

Def.

Cattle
Pen

F.P.

Well

Nannerch
Station

W.M.

G.P.

Nannerch
Lodge

F.B.

C.B.

C

Denbigh ⎫ 10 ⎫ M.S
Mold ⎬ 6 ⎬

S.P

Tai-terfynau

C.S.

Rhyd-y-crogwydd-bach

57.   The station opened on 6th September 1869, along with Rhydymwyn. It is near the start of a six-mile long descent and is almost 500ft above sea level. Demolition of all in sight was due to road realignment. (Lens of Sutton coll.)

58.   The eight-lever ground frame is indistinct at the left end of the fence; it lasted in use until 12th May 1962. On the left is the short siding to the cattle dock. (P.Laming coll.)

59.　　The up platform was recorded on 28th August 1961, along with its unusual flower tub. In the distance is the goods yard, which was in use until 30th April 1962. (W.G.Rear/Bentley coll.)

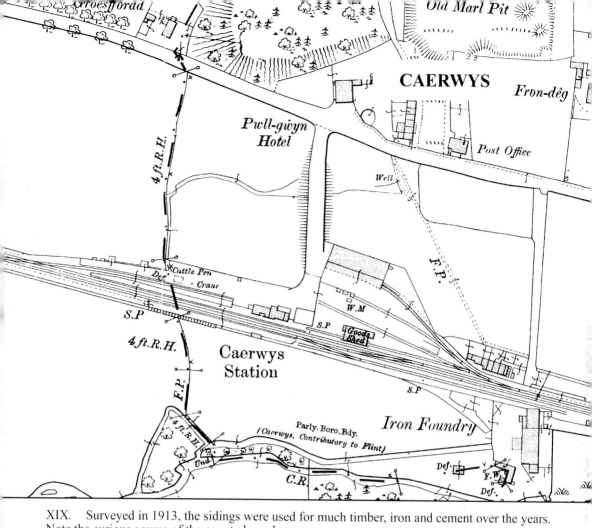

XIX. Surveyed in 1913, the sidings were used for much timber, iron and cement over the years. Note the curious course of the county boundary.

60. The village was one mile north of the station, the community close to it being known as Afonwen. A combined population was 739 in 1901. The pulley of the 5-ton crane is included. (Lens of Sutton coll.)

61.　　A picture from October 1961 shows that the valley is widening on our descent. The goods office is beyond the loading gauge. Westbound passengers had to cross in front of the train. (A.M.Davies)

62.　　Low platforms are evident again, as we witness the descent of the train in April 1962. An 8-lever ground frame was in use on the platform until 30th April 1962, when all traffic ceased. There were three other smaller such frames nearby. (A.M.Davies)

EAST OF BODFARI

63.   A Chester to Denbigh train is approaching Bodfari station in May 1947, behind an ex-LNWR 2-4-2T. The private siding had carried large quantities of limestone for the Partington Iron & Steel Company of Irlam, Lancashire, but the traffic had ceased in 1932. (M.Whitehouse coll.)

CHESTER, MOLD, DENBIGH, RUTHIN, and CORWEN.

January 1935

Down. — Week Days — Suns.

Stations: Chester (General) dep., Saltney Ferry A, Broughton & Bretton, Kinnerton, Hope and Penyffordd, Hope (Exchange) 924, Padeswood & Buckley, Llong, Mold (below), Rhydymwyn, Star Crossing, Nannerch, Caerwys, Bodfari, Denbigh 495 arr./dep., Llanrhaiadr, Rhewl, Ruthin, Eyarth, Nantclwyd, Derwen, Gwyddelwern, Corwen 148 arr.

Up. — Week Days

Stations: Corwen dep., Gwyddelwern, Derwen, Nantclwyd, Eyarth, Ruthin, Rhewl, Llanrhaiadr, Denbigh 495 arr./dep., Bodfari, Caerwys, Nannerch, Star Crossing, Rhydymwyn, Mold (below), Llong, Padeswood & Buckley, Hope (Exchange) 924, Hope and Penyffordd, Kinnerton, Broughton & Bretton, Saltney Ferry A, Chester B 498, 503 arr.

BODFARI

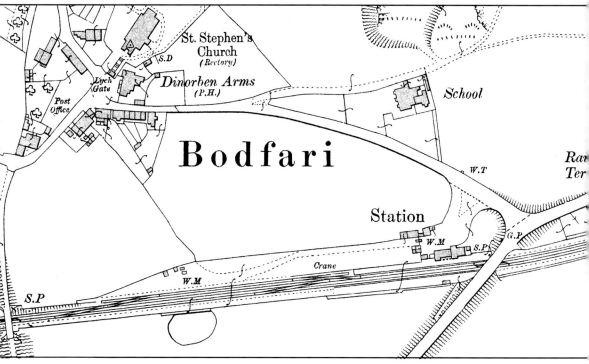

XX.   This extract is from the 1912 edition and it includes one of the many limestone quarries in the area.

64.   There is evidence of timber traffic in this postcard view of the village and its church. The square base of the parcel weighing machine can be seen under the canopy. (Lens of Sutton coll.)

65.   The exit from the down platform was via the path to the gate. The minimal facilities were photographed on 27th August 1954. (R.M.Casserley)

66.   The route to Denbigh from the points in the distance was single from 28th April 1957. This westward panorama is from 20th May 1961 and includes a choice of crossings for passengers. Only the base of the 5-ton crane remains. (B.W.L.Brooksbank)

67.   The parcels shed obscures part of the roofless area for gentlemen; ladies used the area below the first slated roof. A green flag is being held out on 18th September 1961. (Bentley coll.)

68.   This panorama is from the village in May 1962, just after buses had taken over the service. The background is enhanced by the Clwydian Range. (A.M.Davies)

3. From Corwen
CORWEN

69.	The line from Ruabon and Llangollen is on the right and on the other single line is LMS class 2P 4-4-0 no. 675 with the 5.12 from Denbigh on 7th August 1948. The rods on the left ran back to the 25-lever East Box, which was on the up platform and on the left of the next picture. (W.A.Camwell/SLS)

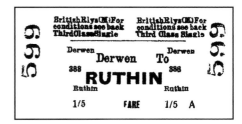

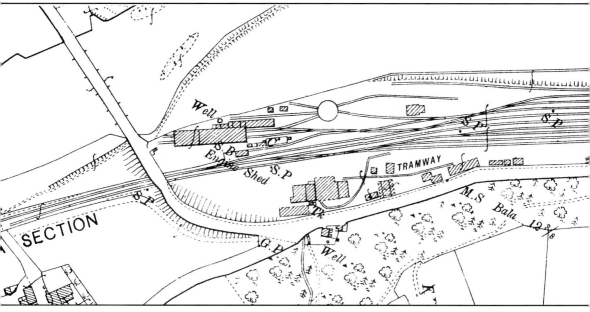

XXI.   The 1911 edition has the GWR single line to Bala Junction on the left. The LNWR/GWR junction is beyond the right border and is illustrated in picture 69. A terminus for trains from Denbigh opened on 6th October 1864 and was on the right. It was temporary, as the station shown came into use in August 1865.

70.   The route was often busy with holiday trains between the Cambrian Coast and the urban areas of the North of England. Thus, lengthy passing facilities were available. Passenger trains from Denbigh arrived on the right, but freights ran through on the left. The picture is from August 1949. (P.J.Garland/R.S.Carpenter)

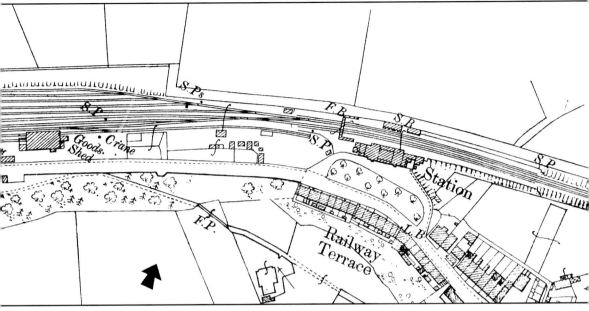

71.   The West Box was recorded in 1952, along with the shear legs in front of it for timber loading. A pit behind it indicates the position of the engine shed, which was a joint GWR/LNWR operation and closed in 1927. However, three LMS crews continued to sign on here. Near the water tank is a turntable and centre is the west end of the goods shed, beyond which was the crane. (W.G.Rear/Bentley coll.)

72.   The 2.05pm Land Cruise train from Rhyl reversed here on 13th August 1953 and 2-6-4T no. 42595 is about to run-round, before returning via Llangollen and Chester. The line across Wales closed before planned, due to flooding on 12th December 1964. The Bala Junction-Llangollen section never reopened. (H.C.Casserley)

Other views of this station are in pictures 44 to 52 in our *Ruabon to Barmouth* album.

Table 100 CHESTER, MOLD, DENBIGH, RUTHIN, and CORWEN

Week Days only

Station	a.m	a.m	a.m	a.m	a.m	a.m	p.m	p.m	S	E		p.m	E	p.m	pm	S	p.m	p.m	p.m		p.m	p.m
Chester (General).......dep	..	..	5 40	7 20	9 6	10 25	D	S	12 45	1 30	..	..	3 45	..	E	4 25	5 42	6 20	8 25	..	..	9 32
Saltney Ferry (Mold Jct.)..	..	..	5 47	7 27	9 6	10 31	..	..	12 51	1 36	..	..	3 51	..	..	4 31	5 49	6 27	8 32	..	..	9 42
Broughton and Bretton......	..	..	5 51	7 32	9 10	10 35	..	..	12 55	1 40	..	..	3 55	..	..	4 35	5 53	6 31	8 36	..	..	9 46
Kinnerton............	..	..	..	7 37	9 15	10 40	..	..	1 0	1 45	..	..	4 0	..	..	4 46	5 58	6 36	8 41	..	..	9 51
Hope and Penyffordd......	..	..	..	7 42	9 20	10 51	..	..	1 11	1 56	..	..	4 11	..	..	4 51	6 8	6 46	8 52	..	..	10 2
Hope (Exchange)......	..	..	6 11	7 52	9 29	10 54	..	..	1 14	1 59	..	..	4 16	..	..	4 54	6 11	6 51	..	..	..	..
Padeswood and Buckley......	..	..	..	7 55	9 32	10 57	..	..	1 17	2 2	..	..	4 18	..	..	4 57	6 14	6 54	8 56	..	..	10 6
Lleng............	..	..	..	7 59	9 35	11 0	..	..	1 20	2 5	..	..	4 22	..	..	5 0	6 17	6 57	..	..	..	..
Mold............	..	..	6 35	8 0	9 41	11 6	..	12 50	1 27	2 13	..	..	4 27	..	5 5	6 6	6 24	7 5	9 5	..	..	10 16
Rhydymwyn......	..	6 45	8 16	9 48	11 13	..	1	1 11	3 42	2 20	..	..	4 34	..	5 11	5 13	6 31	7 12	9 12	..	..	10 23
Star Crossing......	..	..	..	..	11 20	..	1	8 1	41	2 27	..	..	4 41	..	5 18	5 20	6 38	..	9 19	..	..	..
Nannerch......	..	..	8 24	9 57	11 24	..	1	12 1	45	2 31	..	..	4 45	..	5 22	5 24	6 42	7 20	9 23	..	..	10 31
Caerwys............	..	..	8 31	10 4	11 31	..	1	19 1	52	2 38	..	..	4 52	..	5 29	5 31	6 49	7 27	9 30	..	..	10 38
Bodfari............	..	..	7 5	8 39	10 11	11 38	..	1	26 1	58	2 45	..	..	4 59	..	5 36	5 38	6 54	7 33	9 37	..	..	10 44
Denbigh............arr	..	..	7 12	8 47	10 19	11 46	..	1	34 2	6 2	53	..	..	5 7	..	5 45	5 49	7 2	7 45	9 45	..	..	10 52
Denbigh............ dep	6	5 6	25	7 22	9 16	..	9 2	5	12 50	..	..	..	3 45	5 12	..	..	..	7 54	..	10 7	..
Llanrhaiadr......	6	34	7 31	9 21	..	9 21	12 56	..	..	..	3 51	5 18	..	..	..	8 0	..	10 13	..
Rhewl............	6	36	7 36	9 21	..	9 21	1 1	..	..	..	..	5 23	..	..	..	8 5	..	10 18	..
Ruthin............	6 16	76 07	7 40	9 26	..	9 21	1 5	..	..	..	4 1	5 32	..	..	..	8 10	..	10 20	..
Eyarth............	..	..	8 32	9 27	..	..	..	..	4 7	5 37	..	..	..	8 16	..	10 28	..
Nantclwyd......	7 12	..	8 39	9 34	..	..	..	..	4 14	5 43	..	..	..	8 25	..	10 37	..
Derwen............	..	..	9 45	9 40	..	..	..	..	4 20	5 52	..	..	..	8 31	..	10 43	..
Gwyddelwern......	7 25	..	9 52	9 47	..	..	..	..	4 27	6 0	..	..	..	8 33	..	10 50	..
Corwen............arr	7 33	..	9 59	9 54	..	..	..	..	4 34	6 7	..	..	..	8 45	..	10 57	..

73.   The train shown in the last picture is seen shortly before arrival at Corwen. It is seen from the rear coach as the locomotive approaches the six-span lattice bridge over the River Dee. This was eventually demolished. Nearby had been a siding for E.Jones & Sons, between about 1904 and 1947. (H.C.Casserley)

Miles		a.m	a.m	a.m		a.m	a.m	a.m		p.m	p.m	p.m	p.m	p.m	p.m	p.m	p.m		p.m		p.m		
	Week Days only																						
	Corwen............dep	..	..	..	..	5 10	..	1110	..	..	D	2 25	E	4 58	E	..	6 48	..	9 15	..	..
2½	Gwyddelwern.........	..	..	..	..	5 16	..	1116	..	..	..	2 31	..	5 6	..	..	6 56	..	9 23	..	..
5	Derwen............	..	..	..	..	5 22	..	1122	..	..	..	2 37	..	5 12	..	..	7 2	..	9 29	..	..
7½	Nantclwyd.........	..	..	..	..	5 27	..	1127	..	..	..	2 42	..	5 17	..	..	7 7	..	9 34	..	..
10½	Eyarth............	..	..	..	..	5 34	..	1134	..	..	..	2 49	..	5 24	..	..	7 14	..	9 41	..	..
12	Ruthin............	..	6 45	7 30	..	5 40	9 22	1140	..	..	1 20	2 55	..	5 30	..	..	7 20	..	9 47	..	..
13½	Rhewl............	..	6 48	7 53	..	5 44	9 31	1144	..	..	1 23	2 59	..	5 34	..	..	7 24	..	9 51	..	..
16	Llanrhaiadr......	..	6 55	7 58½	..	5 50	9 36	1150	..	..	1 29	3 5	..	5 39	..	..	7 30	..	9 57	..	..
18½	Denbigh....{ arr	..	7 2½	8 6	..	5 59	9 43	1159	..	..	1 38	3 12	..	5 46	..	..	7 37	..	10 6	..	..
	{ dep	..	7 15	8 11	..	9 48	12 5	..	12 50	..	3 22	4 15	4 55	..	5 59	..	7 43	..	..	..	..
22½	Bodfari...........	..	7 23	8 18	..	9 55	1212	..	1257	..	3 29	4 22	5 2	..	5 57	..	7 50	..	..	..	..
25	Caerwys..........	..	7 29	8 25	..	10 2	1219	..	1 4	..	3 36	4 29	5 9	..	6 4	..	7 57	..	..	..	..
28½	Nannerch.........	..	7 37	8 33	..	1010	1227	..	1 12	..	3 44	4 37	5 17	..	6 12	..	8 4	..	..	..	..
29½	Star Crossing.....	..	..	8 37	..	1014	..	..	1 16	..	3 48	..	..	..	..	..	8 9	..	..	..	..
31½	Rhydymwyn.......	..	7 44	8 42	..	1019	1234	..	1 21	..	3 53	4 45	5 25	..	6 19	..	8 14	..	..	..	..
34½	Mold............	7 10	7 52	8 49	..	1025	1243	..	1 29	..	4 1	4 51	5 36	..	6 27	..	8 23	..	..	..	..
36½	Llong............	7 15	7 56	8 53	..	1030	1247	..	1 33	..	4 5	..	5 40	..	6 30	..	8 27	..	..	..	..
37	Padeswood and Buckley...	7 21	7 59	8 56	..	1033	1249	..	1 36	..	4 8	..	5 43	..	6 34	..	8 30	..	..	..	..
38½	Hope (Exchange)........	7 28	..	..	..	1037	1253	..	1 40	..	4 12	..	5 46	..	6 38	..	..	..	..	..	..
39	Hope and Penyffordd...	7 30	8 49	9 1	..	1039	1255	..	1 42	..	4 14	..	5 48	..	6 40	..	8 36	..	..	..	..
41½	Kinnerton.........	7 35	9 9	9 16	..	1044	1 0	..	1 47	..	4 19	..	5 53	..	6 45	..	8 41	..	..	..	..
43½	Broughton and Bretton...	7 40	9 14	9 10	..	1048	1 4	..	1 51	..	4 23	..	5 57	..	6 49	..	8 45	..	..	..	..
44½	Saltney Ferry (Mold Jct.)...	7 44	9 16	9 16	..	1052	1 9	..	1 56	..	4 27	..	6 2	..	6 54	..	8 50	..	..	..	..
48	Chester (General)......arr	7 52	9 29	9 25	..	11 3	1 15	..	2 4	..	4 35	..	6 11	..	7 2	..	8 58	..	..	..	..

A Calls to set down only.   B 3 minutes later on Saturdays.   C Arr. 5 minutes *earlier*.
D Thursdays and Saturdays.   E Except Saturdays.   F Arr. 6 40 a.m.   S or §Saturdays only.
V Arr. 6 20 a.m.

September 1952

GWYDDELWERN

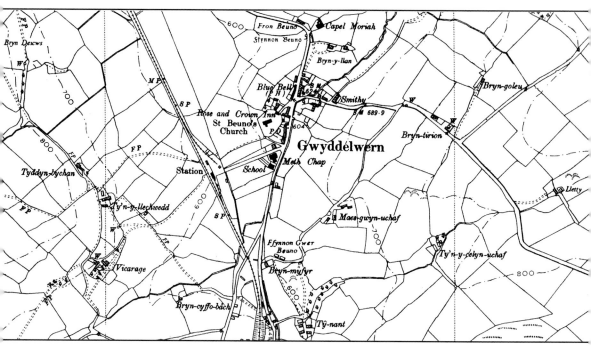

XXII.   The 1952 edition at 6ins to 1 mile reveals that the tiny village has two pubs, two chapels and one church, but the station was a little remote. The siding had earlier continued south to rejoin the running line.

74.   Mynydd Rhyd-ddu enhances this northward panorama from 13th August 1953, six months after regular passenger service had ceased on the route. Freight continued here until 2nd December 1957. Further north were the 1924 sidings for the Craig-Lelo Quarry Co. and the 1891 ones for the Dee Clwyd Granite Quarries Co. The station had a 6-lever frame on the platform, with instruments in the office. (H.C.Casserley)

DERWEN

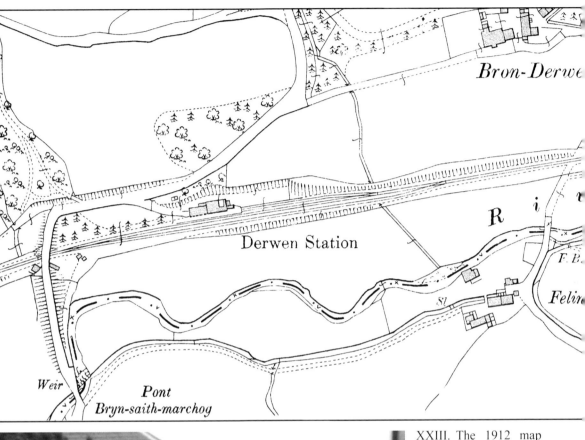

Weir

Pont
Bryn-saith-marchog

Derwen Station

Bron-Derwe

R i

F.B.

Feli

XXIII. The 1912 map has high ground at the top and the county boundary running along the infant River Clwyd, which flows east here.

75. A snap from a window on 13th August 1953 is from a southbound train. The gradient rises behind the camera for one mile to the summit, which was over 600ft above sea level. (H.C.Casserley)

76.   More fine scenery can be enjoyed in three pictures from March 1962. The siding had earlier been a loop - see map. (A.M.Davies)

77.   The local population was 475 in 1901, this dropping to 349 in 1961. The village was ½ mile to the north, but about 300ft higher. The locomotive is 4-6-0 no. 75054. (A.M.Davies)

78.   A small amount of coal traffic continued to be handled here until line closure, but general goods had ceased in December 1957. (A.M.Davies)

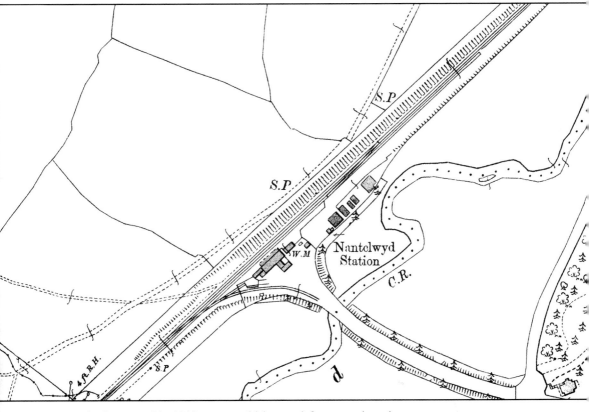

XXIV. The loop on this 1913 map could be used for a goods train to pass a passenger one or another goods. The meandering waterway is the River Clwyd.

79.   The only dwelling nearby was Nantclwyd Hall and the station complemented its fine appearance, apart from the platform face. Few could see it. (Lens of Sutton coll.)

80.   Looking southwest in about 1939, we see the first signals since leaving Corwen. It seems that the loop line was not used for local traffic. On the left is the 8-lever signal frame, which was in use until 2nd July 1955. (Stations UK)

81.   The gates of the private siding are seen from a departing train on 13th August 1953. The buildings were demolished after closure. Goods traffic continued until 2nd December 1957 and coal to 30th April 1962. The canopy had vanished by 1961. (R.M.Casserley)

EYARTH

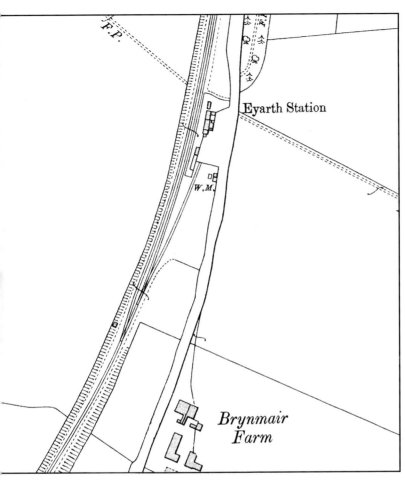

Eyarth Station

W.M.

Brynmair
Farm

XXV. Eyarth Hall and Eyarth House were the main residences in the vicinity of the station. Beyond the right border of this 1912 extract was the small village of Llanfair Dyffryn Clwyd, accessible by the footpath shown.

82.   A resident station master and two porters were provided here for many years. There was no lever frame on the platform or any signals.
(Stations UK)

83.   This is the scene six months after the last regular passenger train had left in 1953. The furthest building was the parcels shed and the nearest was described as the waiting room. The ventilators suggest that it included the toilets; it is seen in August 1953. (H.C.Casserley)

84.   A 1961 view shows all, except the fence, to be in good order. Freight traffic continued here until 30th April 1962 and the loop could be used until 26th June 1965. Later the building was to become a hotel and restaurant and was still so in 2012. (Stations UK)

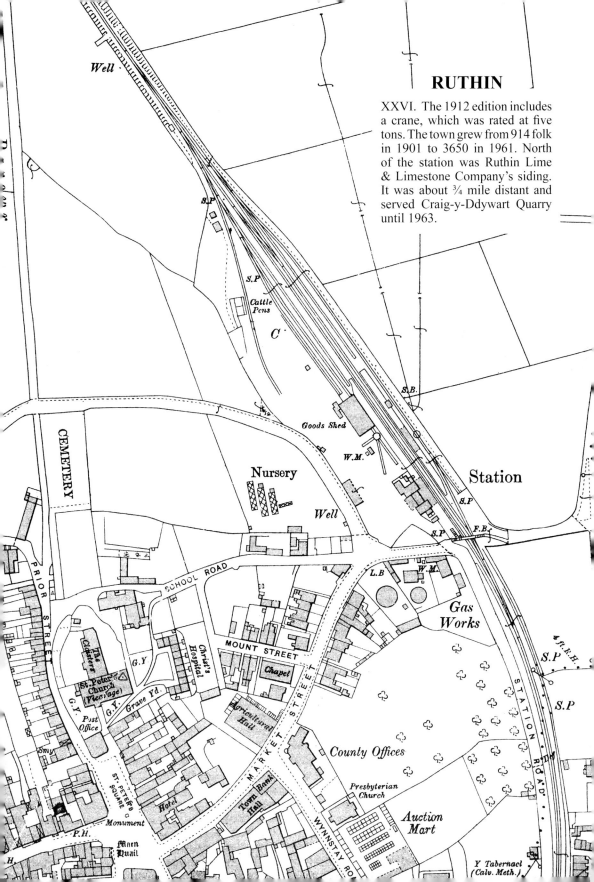

RUTHIN

XXVI. The 1912 edition includes a crane, which was rated at five tons. The town grew from 914 folk in 1901 to 3650 in 1961. North of the station was Ruthin Lime & Limestone Company's siding. It was about ¾ mile distant and served Craig-y-Ddywart Quarry until 1963.

Well

S.P

S.P

Cattle Pens

C

S.B.

Goods Shed

W.M.

Station

Nursery

Well

S.P

CEMETERY

S.P

F.B.

SCHOOL ROAD

L.B

W.M.

PRIOR STREET

Gas Works

4 ft.R.H.

S.P

MOUNT STREET

Christ's Hospital

G.Y

The Cloisters

St. Peter's Church (Vicarage)

Chapel

S.P

STATION ROAD

G.Y

G.Y

Grave Yd.

Post Office

Agricultural Hall

MARKET STREET

County Offices

Smy

St. Peter's Square

Hotel

Town Bank Hall

Presbyterian Church

Monument

P.H.

Maen Huail

WYNNSTAY RO

Auction Mart

Y Tabernacl (Calv. Meth.)

85. A postcard view along Market Street includes many dormer windows and has the station at the far end. The canopy over the entrance was appropriate for a market town. There had been an engine shed here in the early years, but shown on only one map edition. (P.Laming coll.)

➔ 86. A generous canopy was provided on the up platform; the down side was little used by passengers, except on the infrequent occasions when trains passed here. This photograph is from 1939 and includes the signal box on the down platform. It had 22 levers, but only 15 were in use. (Stations UK)

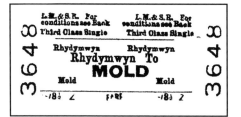

➔ 87. Blowing off on 27th May 1947 is 2-4-2T no. 6712, which is heading the 3.45pm Denbigh to Corwen. The spacious building was planned as the headquarters of the DR&CR. The roof of the goods shed is above the steam. (M.Whitehouse coll.)

88.	A 1956 record includes the footbridge in the background. This did not link the platforms but served locals as a footpath connection. All regular trains had terminated here since 1953; one is to be seen on the front cover. (Stations UK)

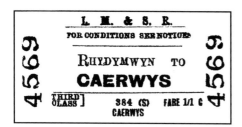

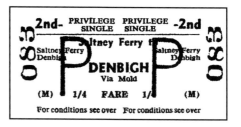

89. The canopy did not reach the platform edge after about 1954, but gas lighting continued to the end. Passenger traffic ceased on 30th April 1962 and goods on 1st March 1965, when the signal box also closed. (E.Wilmshurst)

90. The fine west elevation was photographed in May 1961, but the splendid structure was later demolished to make way for a roundabout. The main road had been the A494 since 1919 and it had a bridge over the line south of the station. (T.J.Edgington)

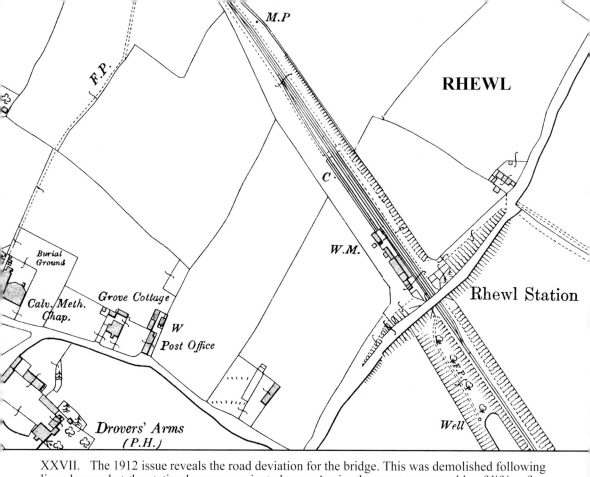

RHEWL

M.P

F.P.

C

W.M.

Rhewl Station

Burial Ground

Calv. Meth. Chap.

Grove Cottage

W
Post Office

Drovers' Arms (P.H.)

Well

XXVII. The 1912 issue reveals the road deviation for the bridge. This was demolished following line closure, but the station became a private house. Again, the crane was capable of lifting five tons. The village centre is close by.

91. Not an ankle to be seen and so this view is probably prior to World War I. The term HALT was used at one period. Ground frames avoided the need for a signal box. (Lens of Sutton coll.)

92.   A photograph from November 1961 shows neglect. Staff had been withdrawn on 1st September 1958, when goods traffic ceased. The canopy had long gone. (A.M.Davies)

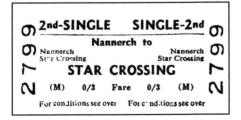

2nd-SINGLE   SINGLE-2nd
Nannerch to
Nannerch   Nannerch
Star Crossing   Star Crossing
STAR CROSSING
(M)   0/3   Fare   0/3   (M)
For conditions see over   For conditions see over

2799   2799

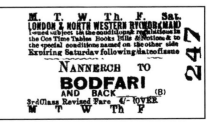

M. T. W. Th. F. Sat.
LONDON & NORTH WESTERN RY(WOR&MAN)
Issued subject to the conditions & regulations in
the Coo Time Tables Books Bills &Notices & to
the special conditions named on the other side
Expiring Saturday following date of issue
NANNERCH   TO
BODFARI
AND   BACK   (B)
3rd Class Revised Fare 4/- OVER
M   T   W   Th   F

247

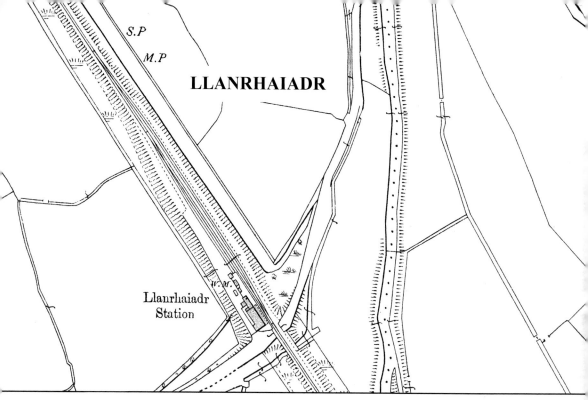

S.P

M.P

LLANRHAIADR

Llanrhaiadr
Station

XXVIII.   The station was 1¼ miles southwest of the small village, on the flat floor of the valley. This is the 1912 survey and little changed.

93.   The low platform of timber construction was retained to the end, unlike most other stations. Those posing are probably staff and relations. Passengers were always few here. (Lens of Sutton coll.)

94.   All traffic ceased here on 2nd February 1953 and this is the scene in 1961. The gates and a two-lever frame had been retained, as had a crossing keeper. All structures were demolished in the 1970s. (Stations UK)

4. Denbigh

XXIX.   The population of the town has fluctuated: 5946 in 1861, 4643 in 1901 and 8130 in 1961, for example. The 1913 edition includes two timber yards, three gas holders and one limeworks (inset).

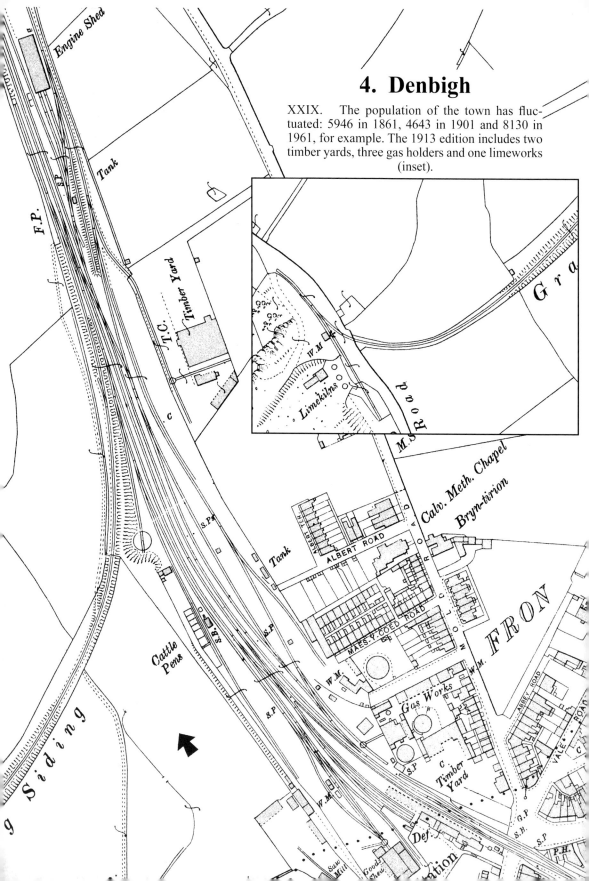

95.   A postcard features the sole through platform, together with a multitude of chimney pots. Much labour was required to keep the fires burning: fortunately this was cheap. The gasworks siding is on the left, together with its turntable. (P.Laming coll.)

96.   LNWR "Precedent" class 2-4-0 no. 1194 *Miranda* was recorded in about 1921; the station is obscured by the cab. On the right are loads of limestone, used as a flux in steel making and dug locally. (W.G.Rear/Bentley coll.)

97.   The train has gone and the smoke has cleared to reveal two cranes and two horses active. The white circles are weighted point levers. (W.G.Rear/Bentley coll.)

98.   The cattle pens were painted white and the lower parts of the cattle wagons were white due to the use of lime wash for reasons of hygiene. On the left is No. 1 Box, which had 38 levers. No. 2 was south of the station and had 15. Both closed on 28th April 1957. (W.G.Rear/Bentley coll.)

99.   On the left is the outline of a coalman near the water tank and coal stage. An LNWR 2-4-2T is departing north in about 1922, destined for Rhyl. Behind the bogie coach are five six-wheelers. (Bentley coll.)

100.   At the same location on 26th September is 2-4-0 no. 1666 *Ariadne,* with the 12.3pm to Chester. The line on the right leads to Graig Quarry. (Bentley coll.)

101.	A gas light was well placed to illuminate the departure boards, the others being in a rack at the bottom of the post. This is the scene on 27th August 1954. (H.C.Casserley)

102.	Looking north on 16th April 1956, we can marvel at the length of the canopy. The short siding had once served a small timber yard. In the distance is No. 1 Box and on the right is the gas works. (R.S.Carpenter)

103. No. 2 Box is out of view in the distance, but we gain a glimpse of the goods sheds on the right. Totem signs had arrived before this photograph was taken on 25th September 1960. (W.G.Rear/ Bentley coll.)

104. Two pictures from September 1961 show the 70-lever box, which opened on 28th April 1957 and replaced the earlier two, plus the one further north at Mold & Denbigh Junction. That had 20 levers and had controlled double track to Denbigh, but this became two single lines thereafter. (W.G.Rear/ Bentley coll.)

105.   The box closed on 19th June 1966, after less than nine years use. All was not lost, as the upper part was removed and used again at Oxley, near Wolverhampton. (W.G.Rear/Bentley coll.)

106.   The engine shed was re-roofed in 1948-49 and was in use until 19th September 1955. The 36ft turntable was on the other side of the running lines in the early years. A 50ft one was behind the shed, in later times. The code was Sub 6K from May 1952. The DMU is working an SLS railtour on 23rd October 1961. (Colour-Rail.com)

107.   Minutes later and the tour participants emerged to examine the details. Locations that afternoon included Coed Talon, Corwen, Rhyl, Prestatyn and Dyserth. (D.K.Jones coll.)

108.   The prospective passenger's perspective was devoid of a clock and spire by 11th May 1967 and their last train had gone by 30th April 1962. The fine building was destroyed in the next decade, when heritage was valued by few. (J.M.Tolson/F.Hornby)

109.   Seen on the same day, the remaining track had become part of the goods yard. Inward traffic included domestic coal and bagged fertiliser, while outward were ferry wagons containing firelighters for Germany, sugar beet and biscuits. Closure came on 1st January 1968. (J.M.Tolson/F.Hornby)

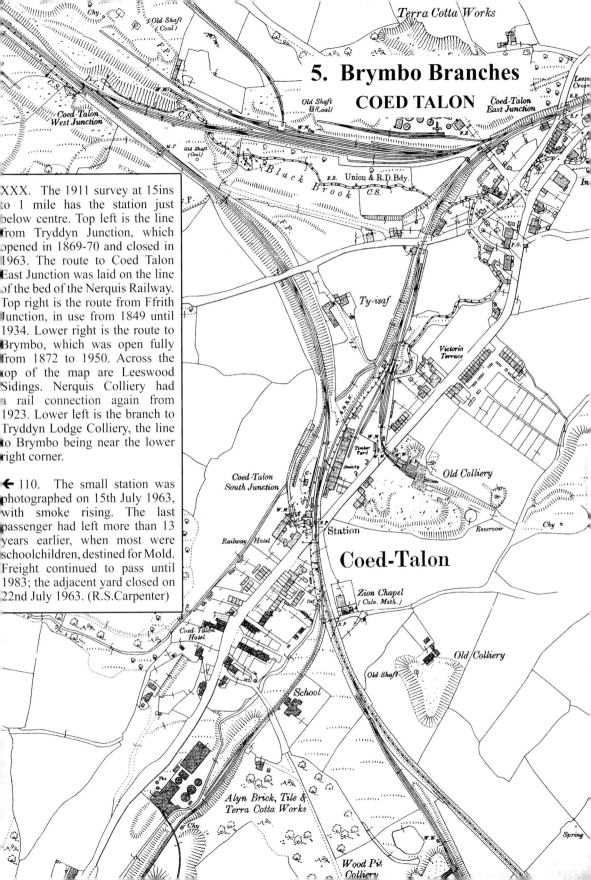

5. Brymbo Branches
COED TALON

Terra Cotta Works

Coed-Talon East Junction

Coed-Talon West Junction

Old Shaft (Coal)

Black Brook

Union & R.D. Bdy.

Ty-isaf

Victoria Terrace

Old Colliery

Coed-Talon South Junction

Reservoir

Timber Yard

Smithy

Station

Railway Hotel

Coed-Talon

Zion Chapel (Calv. Meth.)

Coed-Talon Hotel

Old Colliery

Old Shaft

School

Alyn Brick, Tile & Terra Cotta Works

Wood Pit Colliery

Spring

XXX. The 1911 survey at 15ins to 1 mile has the station just below centre. Top left is the line from Tryddyn Junction, which opened in 1869-70 and closed in 1963. The route to Coed Talon East Junction was laid on the line of the bed of the Nerquis Railway. Top right is the route from Ffrith Junction, in use from 1849 until 1934. Lower right is the route to Brymbo, which was open fully from 1872 to 1950. Across the top of the map are Leeswood Sidings. Nerquis Colliery had a rail connection again from 1923. Lower left is the branch to Tryddyn Lodge Colliery, the line to Brymbo being near the lower right corner.

← 110.   The small station was photographed on 15th July 1963, with smoke rising. The last passenger had left more than 13 years earlier, when most were schoolchildren, destined for Mold. Freight continued to pass until 1983; the adjacent yard closed on 22nd July 1963. (R.S.Carpenter)

LLANFYNYDD

XXXI. This was the northern station on the GWR/LNWR Wrexham and Minera Joint Line. The station opened on 2nd May 1909 and closed on 27th March 1950. The goods yard had a 5-ton crane and closed on 1st May 1952. As late as 1947, there were two sidings further south, serving Crown Dale Colliery and Trimley Hall Colliery.

111. This is part of a postcard of no known date. The small community was nearby, but traffic was light, although the lavatory cistern seems enormous. Income from passengers was £142 in 1903, £53 in 1923 and £10 in 1933. (A.Dudman coll.)

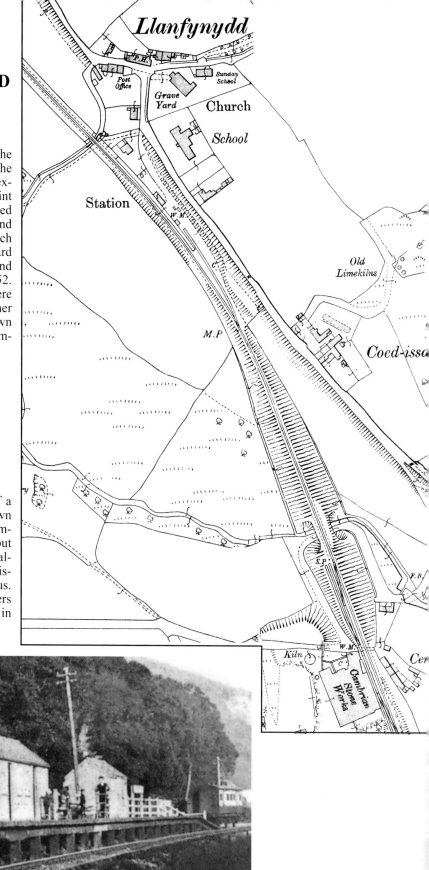

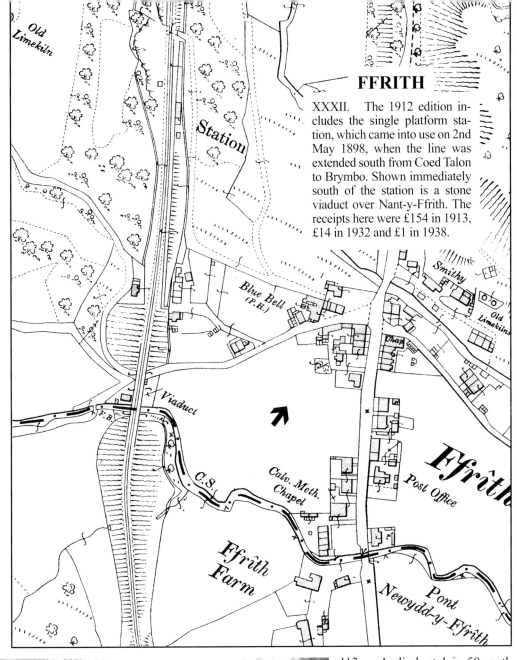

FFRITH

XXXII. The 1912 edition includes the single platform station, which came into use on 2nd May 1898, when the line was extended south from Coed Talon to Brymbo. Shown immediately south of the station is a stone viaduct over Nant-y-Ffrith. The receipts here were £154 in 1913, £14 in 1932 and £1 in 1938.

112. A climb at 1 in 50 south from the station for 1¾ miles brought the route to over 600ft above sea level. Trains were down to one coach when they ceased on 27th March 1950.
(Lens of Sutton coll.)

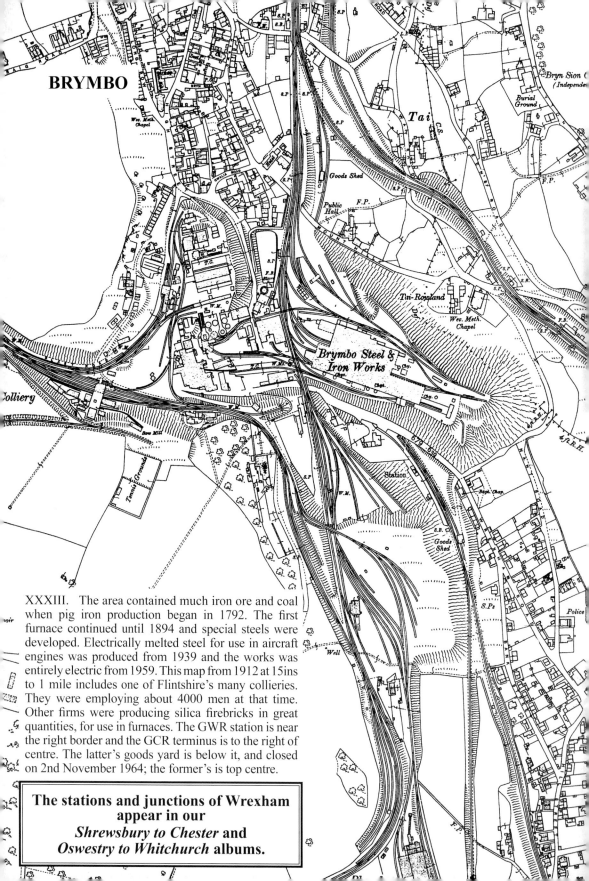

BRYMBO

XXXIII. The area contained much iron ore and coal when pig iron production began in 1792. The first furnace continued until 1894 and special steels were developed. Electrically melted steel for use in aircraft engines was produced from 1939 and the works was entirely electric from 1959. This map from 1912 at 15ins to 1 mile includes one of Flintshire's many collieries. They were employing about 4000 men at that time. Other firms were producing silica firebricks in great quantities, for use in furnaces. The GWR station is near the right border and the GCR terminus is to the right of centre. The latter's goods yard is below it, and closed on 2nd November 1964; the former's is top centre.

**The stations and junctions of Wrexham
appear in our
Shrewsbury to Chester and
Oswestry to Whitchurch albums.**

113.   This southward panorama is from the top border of map XXXIII and is from the LNWR/ GWR Joint Railway, which began about ½ mile north of Llanfynydd. Curving to the left is the GWR route to Brymbo station and straight on is its line to Brymbo Steelworks, the chimneys of which are in the background. This route continued to Vron Colliery. It was sunk in 1806 and closed in 1943. Middle Crossing Box is seen on 11th July 1959. (A.Neale coll.)

114.   The GWR premises are on the right in this northward panorama from a postcard. The line passes over Mount Hill, near the signal box. Brymbo had 4610 residents in 1901 and issued 117,843 tickets to GWR passengers in 1913, when there was a staff of 17. This was down to 11-13 in the 1930s. (A.Dudman coll.)

115. Seen on 15th May 1948, the buildings were later demolished. They had been GWR property, but were used by the LNWR and its successors. Trains from Wrexham had ceased in 1931, when there was a staff of 15 listed by the GWR. (R.G.Nelson/T.Walsh)

116. Part of the Brymbo Steelworks was photographed in July 1957, with one ex-GWR signal post still standing on the left. Rail traffic ceased on 1st October 1983 and the works closed in September 1990, the internal railway being in use to the end. (A.Neale coll.)

THE LODGE HALT

117.   This was the next stop south of Brymbo and the GWR provided a passenger service from 1st July 1906 to 1st January 1931. The district is still known as The Lodge. (Stations UK)

PLAS POWER

118.   The GWR station was recorded on a quality postcard. It served passengers from February 1883 until 1st January 1931. To the west was another station of the same name and that was opened by the WM&CQR on 1st August 1889 and closed by the GCR on 1st March 1917. The GWR staff numbered seven in 1923 and four in 1929; the goods yard closed on 2nd April 1956. (Stations UK)

WEST OF WREXHAM

119.   This is Croes Newydd Yard which served as the Minera Branch Yard and is viewed on 16th November 1961, facing the main line. The 0-6-2Ts are nos. 6617 (left) and 6674. There had been a passenger service from Wrexham using railmotors from 1st May 1905 until 1st January 1931, apart from two of the war years, the terminus being Berwig Halt. (R.G.Nash/T.Walsh coll.)

120.   A view in the other direction on the same day from the east end of the yard has the wagon repair facilities on the left. In the distance is Croes Newydd West Box and the long building on the right accommodated the offices for the yard master, the goods agent, the goods clerks and the weighbridge. (R.G.Nash/T.Walsh coll.)

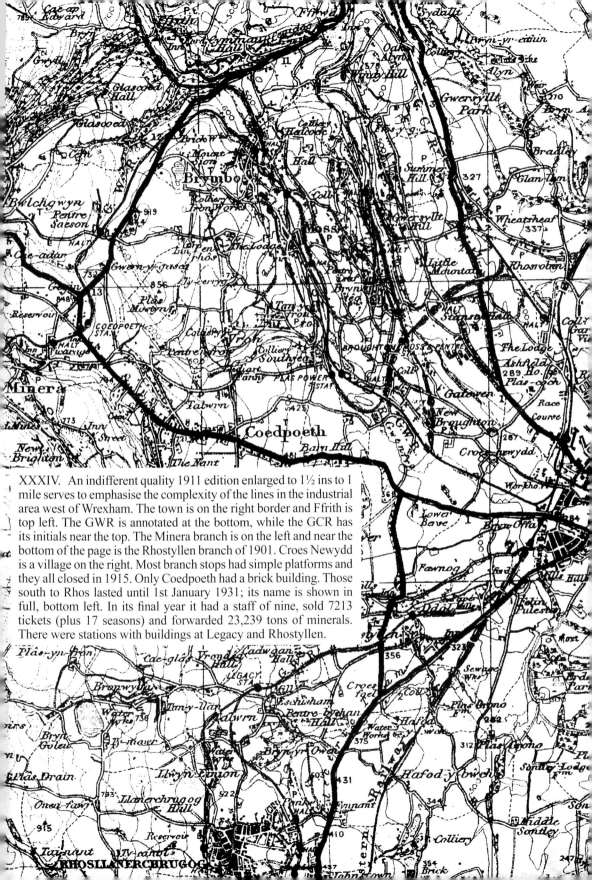

XXXIV. An indifferent quality 1911 edition enlarged to 1½ ins to 1 mile serves to emphasise the complexity of the lines in the industrial area west of Wrexham. The town is on the right border and Ffrith is top left. The GWR is annotated at the bottom, while the GCR has its initials near the top. The Minera branch is on the left and near the bottom of the page is the Rhostyllen branch of 1901. Croes Newydd is a village on the right. Most branch stops had simple platforms and they all closed in 1915. Only Coedpoeth had a brick building. Those south to Rhos lasted until 1st January 1931; its name is shown in full, bottom left. In its final year it had a staff of nine, sold 7213 tickets (plus 17 seasons) and forwarded 23,239 tons of minerals. There were stations with buildings at Legacy and Rhostyllen.

MP Middleton Press

EVOLVING THE ULTIMATE RAIL ENCYCLOPEDIA

Easebourne Lane, Midhurst, West Sussex.
GU29 9AZ   Tel:01730 813169

www.middletonpress.co.uk   email:info@middletonpress.co.uk
A-978 0 906520 B- 978 1 873793 C- 978 1 901706 D-978 1 904474
E - 978 1 906008   F - 978 1 908174

All titles listed below were in print at time of publication - please check current availability by looking at our website - **www.middletonpress.co.uk** or by requesting a Brochure which includes our *LATEST* RAILWAY TITLES also our TRAMWAY, TROLLEYBUS, MILITARY and COASTAL series